TOP YOUTUBE STARS™

RHETT MCLAUGHLIN AND LINK NEAL

Comedians with More Than
5 BILLION VIEWS

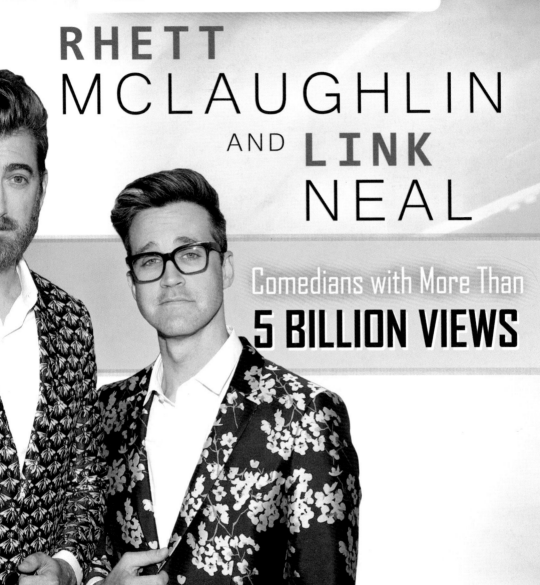

KERRY HINTON

rosen publishing's
rosen central®

New York

Published in 2020 by The Rosen Publishing Group, Inc.
29 East 21st Street, New York, NY 10010

First Edition

Library of Congress Cataloging-in-Publication Data

Names: Hinton, Kerry, author.
Title: Rhett McLaughlin and Link Neal : comedians with more than 5 billion views / Kerry Hinton.
Description: First edition. | New York : Rosen Publishing, 2020. | Series: Top YouTube stars | Includes bibliographical references and index.
Identifiers: LCCN 2019015772| ISBN 9781725348325 (library bound) | ISBN 9781725348318 (pbk.)
Subjects: LCSH: McLaughlin, Rhett—Juvenile literature. | Neal, Link—Juvenile literature. | YouTube (Electronic resource)—Biography—Juvenile literature. | Internet personalities—United States—Biography—Juvenile literature. | Comedians—United States—Biography—Juvenile literature.
Classification: LCC PN1992.9235 H55 2019 | DDC 791.092 [B]—dc23
LC record available at https://lccn.loc.gov/2019015772

Manufactured in the United States of America

On the cover: During the course of their friendship, Rhett and Link have gone from college cutups to walking the red carpet at award shows.

CONTENTS

In the world of YouTube musical comedy, Rhett McLaughlin and Link Neal stand apart. In the words of Lifehacker.com writer Nick Douglass, "They are two of the most famous well-behaved grown adults on YouTube." Even though this is true, Rhett and Link have also attracted millions of subscribers for their funny and playful uploads. This popular comedy duo stays very connected to their fan base through their website, Mythical.com, social media, and YouTube. Like many YouTube celebrities, Rhett and Link are multitalented. They write comedic songs, skits, screenplays, and books. Since their first YouTube upload in 2006, their videos have been viewed over five billion times by their fans across the internet. Rhett and Link's content stretches across four YouTube channels with over twenty-four million subscribers. They also run and oversee Mythical, the entertainment collective and company that produces all of their content.

Aside from these accomplishments, Rhett and Link are also well known in the advertising world. Since 2009, the duo has made humorous commercials for local businesses as well as major international brands, including Taco Bell, McDonald's, and Coca-Cola. Although Rhett and Link are humorous comedians and musicians, their hard work is the real secret of their success. In a world with endless choices for entertainment, they have managed to engage and entertain their subscribers and fans for over fifteen years. Unlike some more controversial YouTube stars, Rhett and Link produce very wholesome content—their comedy is rarely dirty or mean-spirited and has also been instrumental in their accomplishments. Simply put, Rhett and Link are two family men from humble beginnings who have been fortunate enough to make a living through what they love most: music, comedy, and a lifelong friendship.

Through dedication, determination, and a lifelong friendship, Rhett and Link have created a comedy empire followed by millions.

CHAPTER ONE

The First Day of School

Rhett and Link have been creative partners since the day they met. In fact, they can trace their collaborations to an exact date: September 4, 1984. On the first day of first grade, the two young boys were caught writing profanity on their desks. When their teacher, Ms. Locklear, discovered the naughty words, she made Rhett and Link stay inside during recess. Their punishment was coloring pictures of unicorns and other mythical beasts. This story is also told in the YouTube video for the song "How We Met Song (Color a Mythical Beast)." This shared experience created a bond between the two boys, marking the first day of a thirty-year friendship.

THE EARLY, EARLY YEARS

Rhett James McLaughlin was born on October 11, 1977, in Macon, Georgia. His family moved to California when Rhett was a toddler before settling in the small town of Buies (BOO-ees) Creek, North Carolina. Rhett's father taught at nearby Campbell

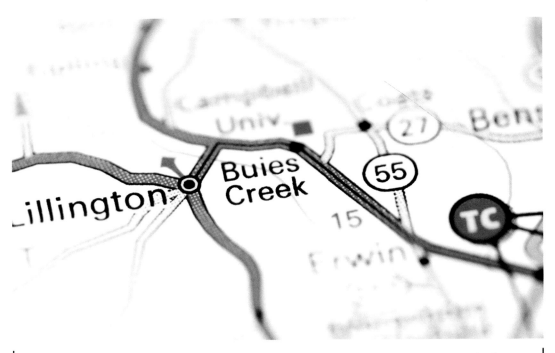

Buies Creek, North Carolina, is Rhett and Link's hometown. The rural community is home to Campbell University and is about 30 miles (48 kilometers) from Raleigh, the capital of North Carolina.

University Law School. Rhett became interested in design at a young age. He was drawing floor plans and blueprints before he turned seven and he wanted to pursue a career as an architect. Rhett was also very active, playing both basketball and soccer.

Link was born Charles Lincoln Neal III on June 1, 1978, in Boone Creek, North Carolina. His parents eventually shortened his middle name into the nickname he is known by today. After Link's parents divorced in 1980, his mother remarried and moved the family to Buies Creek, the same town where Rhett lived. This set the stage for their first meeting. As a boy, Link decided he wanted to be a weatherman after watching the meteorologists on the local news. Strangely, Link was also terrified of lightning

START YOUR OWN YOUTUBE EMPIRE

As performers and comedians, Rhett and Link had humble beginnings. Their first videos were not incredibly professional, but they eventually increased the production quality of their work. Still, this do-it-yourself spirit is a part of their success today.

EQUIPMENT

If you're over the age of thirteen and have a computer and internet access, it's very easy to create your very own YouTube channel. You'll also need a Google account in order to sign up for YouTube. Once that's done, you can create your very own channel where you can upload your videos.

ADDITIONAL GEAR

You'll definitely need a camera to shoot your videos. Cameras range in price and type—you may not need the most expensive gear to start. Using your cell phone, laptop, or desktop to film is the cheapest way to begin. More experienced posters use more professional lighting and external microphones to get better results. For their shows and videos, Rhett and Link use video editing software for a polished look, but YouTube has a free video editor to use. Before you buy anything, ask your parents and do your research. Start with watching your favorite YouTube videos. YouTube celebrities are often interviewed about their gear. Online customer reviews and your local computer store can also provide good advice.

RECORD!

Making great videos is obviously not this simple, but the steps to get there are very clear. Creating a channel and attracting subscribers require enough content for people to come back and see your new work. Many popular videos are well-planned and scripted before a camera records the first frame of video. Before you show your work to the world, be sure to have a product you can be proud of.

throughout his childhood. In the YouTube video "People Struck by Lightning Who Lived," Rhett calls this situation "the weatherman's dilemma."

STARTING EARLY

After coloring their first unicorns, Rhett and Link continued to collaborate on media projects. Both boys loved listening to the

Rhett and Link's elementary school experiences have affected their comedy to this day. They even made a documentary about their beloved teacher Ms. Locklear. Link is seen here third from right in the first row and Rhett is third from right in the top row.

radio, comedy, and impersonations. When they were ten, the two began recording a series of audio skits. In the recordings, Rhett and Link did impersonations of different characters in between songs recorded from the radio. In the 2012 YouTube video "Secret Tapes of Rhett & Link," the duo played an interview skit from one of the last remaining cassettes they have.

FIRST NOTES

Both Rhett and Link had their first experience with musical instruments in the fourth grade. Like many of the milestones of their friendship, Rhett and Link learned the recorder from the same teacher. Although the two weren't especially gifted, the lessons sparked a lifelong love for making music.

Rhett and Link continued to play music in middle school. In seventh grade, they passed the musical test required to join the school band. After the test, each boy bought a trumpet. Rhett never had the chance to play—his trumpet was stolen before the first band practice. Link stayed in the band and eventually became second chair on his instrument. Today, Link keeps both his first recorder and trumpet in the same case and often uses them to record music with Rhett. Rhett currently has no idea where his recorder or trumpet may be. Since their first recorder lesson, Rhett has also learned enough piano to use it for songwriting, and Link has added the harmonica to his list of instruments, and possibly to his trumpet case.

CHAPTER TWO

A Friendship Continues

During their years at Hartnett Senior High School, Rhett and Link pursued some separate interests and hobbies while continuing their friendship. Despite a new school and new activities, they always managed to get together to laugh, create, and dream. For the next four years, Rhett and Link would deepen their bond even more.

"GUTLESS WONDERS"

One of the earliest projects Rhett and Link worked on in high school was a screenplay entitled "Gutless Wonders." The twenty-eight-page unfinished script follows fictional versions of our heroes as they make amazing discoveries about Link's dog Tucker. The two find that Tucker can both dress himself and talk, and they book him on the local news. However, Tucker disappears before his big moment. Although Rhett and Link filmed a few scenes, they were lost and only the script remains today. They read the full screenplay for their fans over five episodes of *Good Mythical Morning* in 2012.

In between bouts of scaring cows, Rhett and Link talked about their hopes and dreams in a pasture near Buies Creek.

THE OATH: BLOOD BROTHERS

The creek in Buies Creek was a special place for Rhett and Link. It served as a meeting place, creative laboratory, and place to connect with nature. What also made it attractive to the two was the nearby cow pasture, situated across the creek from a nearby golf course. One of the boys' favorite hobbies was to cross the creek and chase the cows across the grazing field. Rhett and Link have stressed that they do not endorse this behavior today.

At the creek, Rhett and Link would sit on rocks and talk about their futures and dreams. There wasn't much of an arts

Music is an essential part of Rhett and Link's comedy, and they've been composing and playing songs as long as they've been writing comedy routines.

community in Buies Creek, but the boys loved music and movies and knew that they wanted to be creative in some way after high school and college. Rhett and Link had also begun to realize that they loved to perform in front of audiences. Performing in front of people gave them an instant indication of the quality of their jokes and impressions. The two weren't sure of a specific goal, but they knew they wanted to be creative teammates and business partners. In tenth grade, they decided to make their agreement formal. To make this even more formal, Rhett and Link agreed on an unbreakable blood oath to seal the deal. According to Rhett in Episode 22 of *Ear Biscuits*, they vowed, "We're gonna do something awesome and we're gonna do it together."

They wrote the oath down on two pieces of paper and cut their palms with a piece of glass they found in the pasture dirt. Neither Rhett nor Link can recall if they then shook hands. Today, Rhett and Link do not support this type of behavior either. The original copies of the oath are lost to history. Rhett lost his many years ago, and later, Link lost the wallet that contained his. Rhett and Link have touched on this story in their videos on YouTube and also in their 2009 documentary, *Looking for Ms. Locklear.*

WAX PAPER DOGZ

In their junior year of high school, Rhett and Link decided to form a band with two of their friends. None of the boys had any real musical talent, but they refused to let that stop them. They hoped their enthusiasm would be a substitute for skill. Link did not want to play trumpet or recorder; he felt they were more suited for a school orchestra than the band they wanted to start. Both Rhett and Link wanted to be lead singer; being best friends, they decided to share the duties. They named the band Wax Paper Dogz.

The group tried to write a song but realized they didn't really know how. A bandmate's dad suggested they perform cover songs. The dad could play guitar and keyboard, and he wound up teaching the band the basics of music and helped them choose material. The first song the band played was "I Can See Clearly Now" by Johnny Nash. After seeing a video of the Dogz performing for friends, Rhett decided the band needed only one lead singer and he bought a guitar and learned enough to play with the band one month later with Link performing lead vocals on his own. Wax Paper Dogz changed its image over time. The band started playing country music, but within eighteen months

STARTING YOUR OWN BAND

The musical education Rhett and Link received from Wax Paper Dogz is a large part of their success today. Starting a band may not guarantee worldwide fame, but it will give you the chance to collaborate, improve your musical skills, and have fun.

WHO'S IN?

Find out who will be in your band. Ask family members or friends if they'd like to be involved. Never played an instrument? It may be good to take some lessons on your own—relatives or teachers who can play are great to ask for either advice or lessons also. If you already play an instrument, audition for your school band.

WHAT'S PLAYING?

Be democratic—see what the other members want to play. Bands that can agree on material and presentation usually last longer than those that don't.

WHERE TO PLAY?

Practicing can make both a band and individual members better. Finding a place to practice can be difficult. Bands make noise, and not everyone will be excited to hear a new band figuring out how to play. See if your school has some sort of practice space. Your local record store can also be helpful in finding a rehearsal spot.

HEARD THAT?

Your band should document its music. Listening back to what you've played is a great way to learn and hear mistakes. As you're starting, the quality of your recordings doesn't have to be perfect. Demos can be recorded using the built-in microphone on a laptop or cell phone. If you have some money to spend, an external microphone can definitely make your songs sound more professional.

turned into a rap-rock band. The band eventually expanded into a six-piece group. No live footage of Wax Paper Dogz has survived. The band's song "Red and Yellow, Black and White" was featured on the CD *Why This Way? 3rd Compilation of Independent Bands* in 1997.

MORE THAN MUSIC

Rhett and Link had other interests besides music—sports provided another bond they shared through high school. Link had chosen to play soccer instead of joining the school band. If he hadn't, Wax Paper Dogz may never have formed. Outside of the band, Rhett played multiple sports. He ran cross country and was a member of the golf team, but his best sport was basketball. Rhett was over 6 feet (1.83 meters) by

Rhett's height made him an ideal candidate for playing basketball in high school. When he realized he had a talent for the game, Rhett considered playing in college.

his junior year—today he measures 6 feet 7 inches (2 m)—and had become so talented that he considered playing in college and possibly beyond. His father filmed his games with a video camera to send clips to college recruiters. Rhett eventually decided against a career in basketball—he and Link were having much more fun using the camera to make their own videos. Although he abandoned a life in sports, Rhett still holds the state record for the most three-point shots in a single season (77).

CHAPTER THREE

Career Building

R hett and Link continued to honor their blood oath as they approached their college years. Once again, they managed to pursue their own interests while continuing to collaborate

Syme Hall, a dorm at North Carolina State University in Asheville, North Carolina, was basically a laboratory for Rhett and Link as they refined their comedy while studying.

creatively. As they got older, their families would also play a role in their leap into the world of comedy.

INTO THE FUTURE

Toward the end of high school, Rhett and Link were convinced that they wanted to study film together at the University of North Carolina in Asheville, North Carolina. Rhett's father helped convince the boys to be more practical in case their dreams of creating awesome comedy did not come true. In 1996, the two enrolled as freshmen at another state college, North Carolina

Rhett and Link (and their families) are dedicated fans of the NC State Wolfpack basketball team and try to attend games when they are in North Carolina.

State University in Raleigh. They were roommates at Syme Hall and both chose engineering majors. While Rhett studied civil engineering, Link chose to focus on industrial engineering. When asked why by Emily Tench in an interview with *Technician*, the UNC student newspaper, Link humorously replied, "That is the most direct path to a future in entertainment. That's what my guidance counselor told me."

In college, Rhett and Link kept experimenting with making videos featuring them and their roommate Greg. Some of their earliest fans were fellow members of the Campus Crusade for Christ, a Christian student group. Today, Rhett and Link are still fans of the NC State Wolfpack basketball team—in fact, one of their earliest YouTube uploads involves the team. For his

Family is extremely important to Rhett and Link. Their adventures with their wives and children often find their way into *Good Mythical Morning*.

graduation, Rhett was given his very first computer, which came with video-editing software. This technology gave Rhett and Link the chance to make more professional videos.

Life moved quickly during their university years. Rhett and Link met the women who would become their wives. During sophomore year, Link met Christy—they were married in 2000 while Link was still in college. Rhett met Jessie during his junior year of college, and they became husband and wife in June 2001. In addition to raising families with their partners, these two women would eventually give Rhett and Link the final motivation they needed to become full-time entertainers.

A VERY IMPORTANT WEDDING

Not long after they graduated from North Carolina State, Rhett and Link were asked to perform a song at their roommate Greg's wedding rehearsal dinner. They wrote and played a funny song about Greg for his wife, family, and friends. The audience reaction was really positive. Rhett and Link later re-recorded the song with new lyrics and named it "The Unibrow Song." On the way home, both Rhett's and Link's wives convinced them they should go for it and pursue comedy full-time.

BABY STEPS

Although they both received degrees in engineering, Rhett and Link continued to work on comedic material while working full-time jobs. Rhett graduated from college in 2000—Link completed his studies one year later due to an internship at

COMEDY AND "THE TRAGEDY"

Sharing of both good and bad times is an important reason why Rhett and Link have such a deep personal and professional relationship. One of the worst experiences they shared occurred in January 1999. Rhett, Link, and three of their friends took a trip to a ski resort in Appalachia. Out on the slopes, Link lost control while snowboarding over a jump and was seriously injured, breaking his pelvis. Link also suffered temporary memory loss, which forced him to repeat himself over and over. Comedy can sometimes help people cope with difficult life experiences—Rhett turned this horrible accident into a humorous story called "The Tragedy." The 2009 YouTube video "True Story of Link's Broken Pelvis" contains a phrase Link repeated throughout the day: "Hold on. I'm just coming to. Evidently I've hurt my left hip." This quote has become a favorite for Rhett, Link, and their fans. Rhett also wrote a song about the incident, but it has never been released for fans. One month later, Rhett had his own snowboard accident. He suffered a concussion.

computer company International Business Machines (IBM). After college, Link continued to work for IBM while Rhett obtained an engineering job at a company called Black and Veatch. The duo kept writing and recording music and in 2001 released *Just Mail Us the Grammy*, their first album. The album featured "The Unibrow Song." After two years in the workforce, Rhett and Link decided to abandon their careers and found jobs working as "videographers/speakers/lounge singers" in the North Carolina

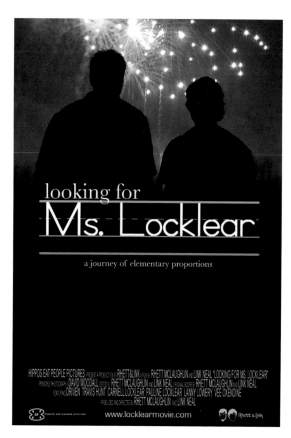

looking for
Ms. Locklear

a journey of elementary proportions

HIPPOS EAT PEOPLE PICTURES PRESENTS A PRODUCTION BY RHETT&LINK A FILM BY RHETT MCLAUGHLIN AND LINK NEAL "LOOKING FOR MS. LOCKLEAR" PRINCIPLE PHOTOGRAPHY DAVID WOODALL EDITED BY RHETT MCLAUGHLIN AND LINK NEAL ORIGINAL SCORE BY RHETT MCLAUGHLIN AND LINK NEAL FEATURING DRIVEN TRAVIS HUNT CARNELL LOCKLEAR PAULINE LOCKLEAR LANNY LOWERY VEE OXENDINE PRODUCED AND DIRECTED BY RHETT MCLAUGHLIN AND LINK NEAL

www.locklearmovie.com   Rhett & Link

Looking for Ms. Locklear showed fans of Rhett and Link's that the two comedians could work in a variety of media types.

Campus Crusade for Christ office. Over the next few years, Rhett and Link would play their videos and perform songs and skits for Christian college students at schools through the southern United States.

Bit by bit, more and more people began to discover Rhett and Link. In December 2005, Rhett and Link released their second album. *I'm Sorry, What Was That? (Live in the Living Room)* was recorded in Rhett's house and includes live versions of "Middle School Girlfriend" and "To Be a Backstreet Boy."

Films came next. In 2006, Rhett and Link released *One Man's Trash*, an eight-minute short film that they entered in film festivals throughout the state. It went on to win "Best North Carolina Comedy" at the All-American Film Festival. That same year, they also began filming *Looking for Ms. Locklear*, a documentary about their first grade teacher. Rhett and Link fully cut their ties to their professional lives in 2007 when they formed a video production company named RhettandLinKreations. A basement in Lillington, North Carolina, served as their studio and company headquarters.

WOLFPACK OR TARHEELS?

When YouTube launched in 2005, Rhett and Link were excited to have a new way to share their comedy with a much wider audience. With their previous experience making videos and sketches, Rhett and Link were prepared. The Rhett & Link channel went live on June 5, 2006. As stated on Mythical.com, "They quickly embraced the platform by populating it with comedy, songs, surreal sketches, and low-budget commercials that went on to become viral sensations." In their first year, Rhett and Link uploaded fifty videos to the Rhett & Link channel. One of them was "Wolfpack or Tarheels?" a short video of Rhett's son Locke reacting to a basketball loss by the North Carolina State Wolfpack against the rival University of North Carolina Tarheels. Initially, Rhett and his wife filmed the clip and uploaded it to rhettandlink.com. The video was shared on YouTube by a viewer, but after it gained thousands of views, Rhett uploaded it to the Rhett & Link YouTube channel. Without even appearing onscreen, Rhett and Link had launched their first viral video.

CHAPTER FOUR

Internetainment

R hett and Link had only begun to scratch the surface of their capabilities as a comedy team. By 2009, they had uploaded around 200 videos with 10 million total views. At this point, their company was very small—Rhett and Link were the only employees. Over the next ten years, they would continue to build on this early success and eventually have ownership and full creative control of a small entertainment empire. By combining the words "internet" and "entertainment," they gave birth to a new term for their brand of comedy: internetainment.

ONLINE NATION

In 2007, Rhett and Link were hired by the CW television network to host a reality television show called *Online Nation*. The show featured random funny and odd internet videos as well as user submitted content. The show planned to allow fans to communicate with one another during live broadcasts, but this never happened since the show was cancelled after only four episodes. Suddenly, Rhett and Link found themselves jobless and without incomes. In the early days of YouTube, making money was not guaranteed.

Rhett and Link's video for AJJ Cornhole launched them into the lucrative world of advertising and led to work with other companies looking for a unique way to promote their products.

Today, YouTube celebrities are paid every time a video is viewed, but in 2007, this was not the case. Rhett and Link refused to be discouraged by the setback. They were forced to discover new ways to support their families and continue their new careers.

COMMERCIAL PRINCES

Rhett and Link began to look to local companies for sponsorship. Their first paid job was a funny music video for AJJ Cornhole, manufacturers of cornhole, a popular outdoor game. The video was viewed millions of times. Rhett and Link's unique approach to commercials brought them to the attention of other advertisers. More commercials followed. In 2009, a credit reporting company called MicroBilt recruited Rhett and Link to film a series of free commercials for local businesses.

I Love Local Commercials was a success. The commercials were done in the style of low-budget local television ads. Many of the ads went viral, including *Butt Drugs*, a spot for an Indiana pharmacy, and one for the Red House Furniture Store in North Carolina.

One of their most famous videos of this era was the 2010 YouTube video *T-SHIRT WAR!!* for a local T-shirt company. Later that year, they repeated the theme in *T-SHIRT WAR 2!!* for McDonald's and Coca-Cola. Rhett and Link continued to make uniquely funny and sometimes silly videos. In 2010, they shot *2 Guys—600 Pillows* for SleepBetter.com. In the commercial, they perform stunts with pillows, and the video is played backward to create an interesting visual effect. Over twenty-four million YouTube viewers loved the video, and it was also awarded the 2011 Webby for Best Editing.

This new line of work gave Rhett and Link the resources to move out of Lillington to new homes and a bigger studio in nearby Fuquay-Varina. Around this time, members of the RhettandLin-Kommunity were deciding what name fans should call themselves. Thousands of fans suggested names. Ultimately, two finalists remained: "RANDLers" (short for Rhett and Linkers) and Mythical Beasts. Rhett liked the second name much more and let subscribers know in video. Today, millions of Mythical Beasts follow Rhett and Link's daily adventures.

COMMERCIAL KINGS

With increased fame from their advertising work, Rhett and Link submitted a television pilot to Independent Film Channel (IFC) in

Rhett and Link's 2011 commercial for Ojai Valley Taxidermy has been viewed more than seventeen million times and launched a meme about the owner, Chuck Testa.

2011. Although IFC did not pick it up, the network offered Rhett and Link their own television series called *Commercial Kings*. Rhett and Link accepted, knowing that this choice required their two families to move to California. With two moving trucks and a minivan, Rhett and Link embarked upon a "Mythical Road Trip" from Fuquay-Varina to Los Angeles. Along the way, they connected with many Mythical Beasts and uploaded two dozen videos documenting the trip. When they arrived, they set up shop in a shed in Rhett's backyard.

Commercial Kings gave viewers the opportunity to watch the duo make local commercials for small businesses around the country. The show had its fans, but IFC decided not to renew the show after the first ten-episode season. The show may have been cancelled, but "Ojai Valley Taxidermy," one of

FUN FUN FACTS

Rhett and Link's fans love to share fun and weird information about their comedy heroes on Reddit and other online forums. For that matter, Rhett and Link also love to share such information about themselves! Here are a few of the more interesting (and verified) facts that have been shared by Rhett and Link in their videos:

RHETT

In the mid 1990s, Rhett submitted an audition tape for the MTV series *The Real World*. He was not chosen.

Rhett's mother, Mama Di, watches every episode of *Good Mythical Morning (GMM)*.

Rhett loves to paddle board and sail.

Rhett's first and only fight was in the third grade in defense of Link.

Rhett's favorite sport to watch is college basketball.

In October 2007, Rhett could be seen sitting on his front porch on Google Street View.

Rhett's favorite musician is the country singer Merle Haggard.

LINK

Favorite singer: Merle Haggard

Favorite animal: Miniature horse

Favorite food: Cereal

Favorite childhood birthday party location: McDonald's

Favorite type of toothpaste: Flavored

Favorite celestial body: LinkStar, a star named after him by Rhett

the commercials for the show went viral after Chuck Testa, the business's owner, uploaded the video to his business You-Tube channel. The video became so popular that the phrase "Nope…Chuck Testa" became an internet meme.

THE FLAGSHIP SHOW

While still living North Carolina, Rhett and Link had begun broadcasting a daily YouTube show called *Good Morning Chia Lincoln*. The "Chia Lincoln" of the title was an Abraham Lincoln Chia Pet that sprouted chia seeds for his face and beard. *Chia Lincoln* ran for about six weeks, but they ended the show after half of

Good Mythical Morning has a weekly spinoff show called *Let's Talk About That* (*LTAT*), which discusses topics and highlights from the previous week's episodes of *GMM*.

the chia sprouts died. After they moved to Los Angeles, they launched a second version of the show. The world saw the first episode of *Good Mythical Morning* on January 12, 2012. Daily episodes of the show average from ten to thirty minutes and are uploaded early in the morning. Rhett and Link are usually found talking about their past, answering viewer mail, and doing weird things with food. Some of the most popular *GMM* episodes focus on food in odd situations. The *Will It?* series explores combining odd ingredients with normal foods, like tacos, ice cream, and milk. Some of Rhett and Link's experiments can be painful. In their "challenge" videos, they eat extremely hot and possibly dangerous items, such as hot peppers and sour food. More than twenty-seven million viewers have watched 2015's "Eating a Scorpion: Bug War Challenge" so far. *Good Mythical Morning* is currently the most watched daily show on the internet.

MORE CHANNELS

Today, Rhett and Link oversee the content for five YouTube channels. The content may vary, but it is all under the shared umbrella of their company, Mythical Entertainment.

RHETT & LINK

Rhett and Link's first channel has nearly five million subscribers. Aside from vlogs, this channel contains most of Rhett and Link's music videos, sketches, and local commercials. The Rhett & Link channel has been inactive since 2017, except for a video promoting *Rhett and Link's Book of Mythicality*.

GOOD MYTHICAL MORNING

This is Rhett and Link's most popular channel since it carries *Good Mythical Morning*, their incredibly popular daily show.

After fifteen seasons, *GMM* averages 100 million views per month and has over fourteen million subscribers. In August 2018, *Let's Talk About That* debuted.

GOOD MYTHICAL MORE

This channel primarily features episodes of *Good Mythical MORE*, the bonus after-show for *GMM*.

MYTHICAL

Mythical was launched on January 22, 2014, as the main YouTube channel for Mythical Entertainment. Originally called This Is Mythical, the channel features food experiments and comedy videos created by popular Mythical staff members, including Jen & John and Lizzie & Ellie.

EAR BISCUITS

Started a few months after Mythical, Ear Biscuits is the home for the video episodes of *Ear Biscuits*, Rhett and Link's weekly podcast.

CHAPTER FIVE

Rhett and Link Today and Tomorrow

When Rhett and Link were recording skits on tape in the 1980s, neither dreamed that their camaraderie and love of comedy would lead to a lucrative career connecting with millions of fans and making them laugh. Rhett and Link have continued expanding their talent to other venues—in the last few years they've created a podcast, written books, and toured to sold out crowds around the world. Today, they employ over forty people at their company, Mythical Entertainment, where they film, write, and perform most of their content.

MYTHICAL ENTERTAINMENT

In 2013, Rhett and Link moved into a new studio in Burbank, California. They quickly outgrew it, and in 2014, they found a new studio. Around the same time, they changed the name of the company from Rhett & Link to Mythical Entertainment. In 2014, Rhett and Link also launched *Good Mythical MORE*, a five- to fifteen-minute show that broadcasts after *GMM*. The videos are less scripted than they are on *GMM*—Rhett and Link usually use the time to discuss whatever

Rhett and Link film portions of their funny music videos and films at the Mythical Entertainment studio in Burbank, California.

may be on their minds. Some topics include "Link's Relationship with Plants," "Rhett's Mumbling Problem," and "Deep Fried iPhone." As of 2019, this channel had nearly four million subscribers.

Rhett and Link's videos continued to attract notice for their quality and comedy. In 2014, they won their second Webby Award for *Breaking Bad: The Middle School Musical*.

WE CAN WORK IT OUT

Over the years, Rhett and Link have worked with other YouTube celebrities. They have appeared in three episodes of *Epic Rap*

Battles of History. One of them, *Mario Bros. vs Wright Bros.,* has been viewed ninety-four million times.

Rhett and Link have also worked with YouTube celebrity comedians such as Tobuscus, the Fine Brothers, and the comedy duo Smosh. Smosh has also guest starred in episodes of *Ear Biscuits* and *The Mythical Show*. In February 2019, Mythical Entertainment purchased Smosh for $10 million in order to allow its founders to keep complete control of both their brand and YouTube channels.

Rhett and Link's work with other networks increased, too. In 2016, they premiered a scripted comedy show on the subscriber service YouTube Red called *Rhett and Link's Buddy System*. All of the episodes were released on the same day and follow the two men as they try to rescue *Good Mythical Morning* from a celebrity who has stolen Rhett's phone to take control of the show. Every episode ends with an original song written especially for the episode. The second eight-episode season was released in 2017.

THE BOOK OF MYTHICALITY

In 2017, Rhett and Link decided to share more about Mythicality with their fans in their first book, *Rhett and Link's Book of Mythicality: A Field Guide to Curiosity, Creativity, and Tomfoolery*. As they state in the opening: "If you decide to read this book, be warned—there is a high likelihood of increased Mythicality in your life, which means you may soon find yourself laughing more, learning more, and not taking yourself too seriously. This mentality has been known to spread easily to your friends and loved ones."

The book reached the top of the *New York Times* best seller list in its first week of sales. In the summer of 2018, Rhett and Link took Mythicality on the road during their Book of Mythicality Tour, performing comedy and songs for their fans in more than twenty cities. The next year, they visited six more, including Toronto, Canada, and Melbourne, Australia. In December 2018, Rhett and Link released a Blu-ray disc that included a performance in Los Angeles and behind-the-scenes tour footage.

FAMILY LIFE

Rhett and Link have made it a point to be creative while maintaining a healthy life outside of work. Although they are so close that one could imagine them still living as roommates back in Syme Hall, Rhett and Link are both family men. Rhett has two children: Shepherd and Locke. Link has three kids: Lillian Grace Neal, Charles Lincoln Neal IV (also nicknamed "Link"), and Lando James Neal. Lando is named for Lando Calrissian, a character from the

Rhett and Link's zany antics, songs, and videos have made them not only wealthy comedians, but also successful businessmen.

Star Wars movie franchise. Rhett's and Link's kids are all close. Locke and Lincoln are best friends, as are Shepherd and Lando. The kids became friends naturally, in the same way as Rhett and Link did. In a 2015 broadcast of *Ear Biscuits*, Rhett and Link joke that these two sets of friends give their fathers "two chances to replace them" and continue their comedy legacy. In reality,

A DAY IN THE LIFE OF RHETT AND LINK

When Rhett and Link first started *Good Mythical Morning*, they had a staff of one. Today, it takes more than forty people to run this comedy engine. With a staff this big, organization and scheduling are two of the keys to success for Mythical Entertainment. Having a real structure in place allows Rhett and Link to create the high-quality content they are famous for.

A typical weekday for Rhett and Link usually begins with filming at least one episode of *GMM*. The number depends on other items in their schedule. They often plan or discuss plans over lunch and spend their afternoons writing more content for their channels and attending planning meetings.

Rhett and Link want their children to choose their own path. As Rhett says, "Don't feel like you have to a YouTube channel, or a website or anything. Just be friends." In addition to raising their families, Rhett's and Link's wives, Jessie and Christy, have appeared in over two dozen Rhett and Link videos. They also co-wrote "Say 'I Love You' Like It's Never Been Said," a chapter in *Rhett and Link's Book of Mythicality*.

MEN OF FAITH

Religion is important to Rhett and Link—their Christian faith influences both the way they live their lives as well as their comedy.

Although they performed songs as the Fabulous Bentley Brothers for JellyTelly, a Christian YouTube channel, in 2009, religion and faith are not often addressed on their own YouTube outlets. As Rhett said in a commencement address at Hartnett Central High School in 2012, "Pursue faith … the key piece in the puzzle of life that, when put into place gives us purpose and meaning." Although they are men of faith, Rhett and Link's material is not religious. They refuse to use their YouTube channels to promote their faith; they would rather make comedy and music for everyone. In 2010, Rhett says the same in a post on the *RhettandLinKommunity* forum: "Yes, Link and I are Christians … and it's a big part of our lives and influences the nature of our content. However, our videos are not Christian, and this Kommunity is not for people of any particular faith … our focus is to make people laugh and bring some light into their lives through our videos. As a result, you're not gonna see us directly address issues of faith through our comedy content."

Rhett and Link have taken their lifelong friendship to creative heights they never imagined. Their shared dream of making awesome things together has come true. This shared love of music and comedy has also enabled them to make a very good living and support their families. Success does not seem to have changed Rhett and Link—they consider themselves the same awkward, music-loving nerds they have been since grade school.

TIMELINE

- 1977 Rhett McLaughlin is born in Macon, Georgia, on October 11.
- 1978 Link Neal is born in Boone Creek, North Carolina, on June 1.
- 1980 Link's family moves to Buies Creek, North Carolina.
- 1984 Rhett's family moves to Buies Creek, North Carolina. On September 1, Rhett and Link meet each other (and Ms. Locklear) in the first grade.
- 1992 Rhett and Link write *Gutless Wonders*.
- 1994 Wax Paper Dogz forms. Rhett and Link make their infamous blood oath.
- 1996 Rhett and Link graduate from Harnett Central High School. In September, Rhett and Link begin freshman year at North Carolina State University.
- 2000 Link marries his girlfriend, Christy, in May.
- 2001 Rhett marries his girlfriend, Jessie, in June.
- 2002 Rhett and Link perform at their friend Greg's wedding rehearsal dinner.
- 2006 Rhett and Link's first YouTube channel, Rhett & Link, is launched on June 5.
- 2007 Rhett uploads *Wolfpack or Tarheels?* to the Rhett & Link channel on March 15.
- 2008 *Good Mythical Morning* is launched on September 17.
- 2013 *Good Mythical MORE* is launched on December 13.
- 2014 Rhett and Link launch Mythical, their fourth YouTube channel. Rhett and Link begin uploading their weekly podcast on their Ear Biscuits channel on March 20.
- 2017 *Rhett and Link's Book of Mythicality*, Rhett and Link's first book, is published on October 13.
- 2019 *The Lost Causes of Bleak Creek*, Rhett and Link's first novel, is published in October.

GLOSSARY

brand A product or service that is recognizable through advertising.

camaraderie Trust and friendliness within a group of friends or coworkers.

collective A group of people working together creatively on a project or goal.

creek A small moving body of water that feeds from a lake or river.

dilemma A situation with two unsatisfactory possible outcomes.

documentary A film or video that focuses on a real subject or situation.

endorse To pay a celebrity or influencer to speak positively about a certain product, website, or brand.

engineering The design and construction of complicated machines or systems.

flagship The most important of a group of things, usually used to describe a noun.

impersonation Pretending to be someone else by imitating his or her voice or another notable quality.

lucrative Making money or wealth.

media The plural of "medium," the methods of communicating with a wide audience. This includes, radio, television, movies, and the internet.

mentality Intelligence.

mythical Something that exists only in the imagination of a group of people.

profanity The use of obscene or dirty words.

recorder A flutelike musical instrument.

second chair The second most talented musician on a specific musical instrument in an orchestra.

sketch comedy A live or filmed comedy performance made up of comedic short scenes, or sketches.

social media Websites or other platforms that connect communities of people online.

tomfoolery Foolish or silly behavior.

viral Spreading across a large segment of the internet very quickly.

vlog A website that contains videos created by a certain person.

wholesome Clean and unoffensive.

FOR MORE INFORMATION

Buffer Festival
Administrative Office
2300 Yonge Street, #1600
Toronto, ON M4P 1E4
Canada
(888) 732-1682
Email:
    support@bufferfestival.com
Website:
    https://bufferfestival.com
Facebook and Twitter:
    @BufferFestival
An annual convention that
    premiers the latest You-
    Tube videos and gives
    awards to creators.

FAN EXPO Canada
20 Eglinton Avenue W, Suite
    1200
PO Box 2055
Toronto, ON M4R 1K8
Canada
(416) 960-9030
Email: info@fanexpohq.com
Website: http://www
    .fanexpocanada.com
Facebook and Twitter:
    @fanexpocanada

Instagram: @officialfxc
FAN EXPO is the third-largest
    pop culture event in North
    America.

The National Comedy Theater
3717 India Street
San Diego, CA 92103
(619) 295-4999
Email: sandiego
    @nationalcomedy.com
Website: https://www
    .nationalcomedy.com
Facebook:
    @NationalComedyTheater
Twitter and Instagram:
    @NCTSanDiego
NCT offers improv perfor-
    mances, classes, and
    summer camps for both
    children and adults.

School of Rock
2101 East El Segundo
    Boulevard, Suite 102
El Segundo, CA 90245
(866) 695-5515
Website: https://www
    .schoolofrock.com

Facebook and Twitter: @SchoolofRockUSA

Instagram: @SchoolofRock

The School of Rock has more than two hundred locations worldwide. They offer individual and band programs for young people, including Rookies (ages six and seven), Rock 101 (ages eight to thirteen), and Performance (ages eight to eighteen).

The Second City Toronto
51 Mercer Street
Toronto, ON M5V 9G9
Canada
(416) 343-0011
Website: https://www .secondcity.com/toronto

Facebook and Twitter: @SecondCityTO

Instagram: @thesecondcity

The Second City is an internationally known improv comedy group with theaters in Chicago, Toronto, and Los Angeles. They offer online classes as well as summer comedy camps for kids and teenagers from ages five to eighteen.

The Streamys
Dick Clark Productions, Inc.
2900 Olympic Boulevard
Santa Monica, CA 90404
(310) 255-4600
Email: support@streamys.org
Website: https://streamys.org

Facebook, Twitter, and Instagram: @streamys

The Streamys are held once a year in Beverly Hills, California. Awards are given in over forty categories at what *Vanity Fair* magazine calls the "Oscars of the Web."

VidCon
PO Box 8147
Missoula, MT 59807
(406) 207-6999
Email: info@vidcon.com
Website: http://vidcon.com

Facebook, Twitter, and Instagram: @VidCon

VidCon is the "world's largest celebration of online video and digital creators." The company has been hosting annual events since 2009 in the United States, England, and Australia.

FOR FURTHER READING

Birley, Shane. *How to Be a Blogger and Vlogger in 10 Easy Lessons: Learn How to Create Your Own Blog, Vlog, or Podcast and Get It Out in the Blogosphere!* Lake Forest, CA: Walter Foster Jr., 2016.

Blomfield, Robert. *How to Make a Movie in 10 Easy Lessons: Learn How to Write, Direct, and Edit Your Own Film Without a Hollywood Budget* (Super Skills). Lake Forest, CA: Walter Foster Jr., 2015.

Ciampa, Rob, and Theresa Moore. *YouTube Channels for Dummies.* Hoboken, NJ: John Wiley & Sons, Inc., 2015.

Kelly, Casey, and David Hodge. *The Complete Idiot's Guide to the Art of Songwriting: Hone Your Craft and Reach for Your Goals—Creative, Commercials, or Both.* New York, NY: Alpha Books, 2011.

Kenney, Karen. *Make and Upload Your Own Videos.* Minneapolis, MN: Lerner Publishing Company, 2018.

Lukas, Lisa Donovan. *The Young Musician's Guide to Songwriting: How to Create Music & Lyrics.* Pacific Palisades, CA: Must Write Music, 2014.

McLaughlin, Rhett, and Link Neal. *The Lost Causes of Bleak Creek: A Novel.* New York, NY: Crown, 2019.

McLaughlin, Rhett, and Link Neal. *Rhett and Link's Book of Mythicality: A Field Guide to Curiosity, Creativity, and Tomfoolery.* New York, NY: Crown Archetype, 2017.

Schroeppel, Tom, and Chuck DeLaney. *The Bare Bones Camera Course for Film and Video.* New York, NY: Allworth Press, 2015.

Smithyman, David, Karen Bergreen, and Jo Grossman. *Young, Funny and Unbalanced: A Stand-Up Comedy Guide for Teens.* Scotts Valley, CA: CreateSpace Independent Publishing Platform, 2012.

BIBLIOGRAPHY

Abbey, Alison. "The Best Parts of Rhett & Link, Plus an Exclusive Interview with the Internet's Kings of Comedy." *Parade*, May 19, 2017. https://parade.com/572574/alison-abbey /the-best-parts-of-rhett-link-plus-an-exclusive-interview -with-the-internets-kings-of-comedy.

Centauromadoose (Victoria Doose). "The Lives of Rhett and Link—Biographic Masterpost." RhettandLinKommunity, May 2, 2015. http://rhettandlinkommunity.com/profiles /blogs/rhett-and-link-s-life-facts-master-post.

Ear Biscuits. "Ep. 22 Rhett & Link 'Childhood.'" Soundcloud, February 28, 2015. https://soundcloud.com/earbiscuits /ep-22-rhett-link-ear-biscuits.

Ear Biscuits. "Ep. 58 Rhett & Link 'Sports.'" Soundcloud, February 27, 2015. https://soundcloud.com/earbiscuits /ep-58-rhett-link-sports-ear-biscuits.

Ear Biscuits. "Ep. 80 Rhett & Link 'Rhett & Link Live.'" Soundcloud, July 31, 2015. https://soundcloud.com/earbiscuits /ep-80-rhett-link-live-ear-biscuits.

Good Mythical Morning. "Gutless Wonders: A Rhett & Link Original Screenplay." YouTube, August 17, 2012. https:// youtu.be/CWgPEsqJDcI.

Good Mythical Morning. "People Struck by Lightning Who Lived." YouTube, February 23, 2016. https://youtu.be/68LWjy7f-tA.

Good Mythical Morning. "Rhett & Link's Musical History." YouTube, August 15, 2012. https://youtu.be/lSjS52xzxJQ.

Good Mythical Morning. "Secret Tapes of Rhett & Link." YouTube, April 3, 2012. https://www.youtube.com/watch ?v=v5itFvGgeqs.

Good Mythical Morning. "True Story of Link's Broken Pelvis."
    YouTube, April 3, 2009. https://youtu.be/p0eiJIgVc9s.

Good Mythical Morning. "Why Our Fans Are Called 'Mythical
    Beasts' - RLVault 15." YouTube, July 27, 2012. https://
    youtu.be/h2Xa5c1JXV4.

Hench, Emily. "Rhett & Link: Questions, Answers and a Whole
    Lot of Bricks." *Technician*, October 11, 2018. http://www
    .technicianonline.com/arts_entertainment/article_bf438a24
    -cd0f-11e8-a6bf-afaf0c9368bd.html.

Ifeanyi, KC. "Inside the 'Mythical Minds' and Digital Empire of You-
    Tube Pioneers Rhett and Link." *Fast Company*, March 29, 2017.
    https://www.fastcompany.com/3069203/rhett-and-link-interview.

JellyTelly. "The Fabulous Bentley Brothers—Genesis." You-
    Tube, January 14, 2009. https://youtu.be/EtWaEJ0dBXI.

McLaughlin, Rhett, and Link Neal. *Rhett and Link's Book of
    Mythicality: A Field Guide to Curiosity, Creativity, and Tom-
    foolery*. New York, NY: Crown Archetype, 2017.

Mythical. "About Us." Retrieved February 5, 2019. https://
    www.mythical.com/about-rhett-and-link.

Rhett & Link. "2 Guys 600 Pillows (Backwards) —Rhett & Link."
    YouTube, December 14, 2010. https://youtu.be/01TL9bUWr6l.

Rhett & Link. "The Cornhole Song." YouTube, December 3,
    2007. https://youtu.be/lo8X4pz_QJ0.

Rhett & Link. "How We Met Song (Color a Mythical Beast)."
    YouTube, February 28, 2013. https://www.youtube.com
    /watch?v=EzxeNtWHpe0.

Rhett & Link. "HS Graduation Speech—Rhett & Link." You-
    Tube, June 12, 2012. https://youtu.be/fuV3R3Ogr9l.

Rhett & Link. "It Begins. (Mythical Road Trip Day 1)." YouTube,
    April 25, 2011. https://youtu.be/d2Tuj2m_dH0.

Rhett & Link. "Looking for Ms. Locklear." YouTube, May 11,
    2012. https://www.youtube.com/watch?v=QGKOCP4Ygsg.

Rhett & Link. "Our TV Show—Rhett & Link: Commercial Kings." YouTube, May 28, 2011. https://youtu.be/Y9ILf_9RpHg.

Rhett & Link. "T-SHIRT WAR!! (stop-motion)—Rhett & Link." YouTube, February 8, 2010. https://youtu.be/DKWdSCt4jGE.

Rhett & Link. "T-SHIRT WAR 2!! (TV Commercial—Stop-motion)." YouTube, May 24, 2010. https://youtu.be/iLoA6BpUWqQ.

Rhett and Link—Topic. "The Unibrow Song." YouTube, November 17, 2015. https://youtu.be/PGWhTTUbCuk.

Shabaz (Rhett McLaughlin). "I heard from my cousin you two are Christians..." RhettandLinKommunity, May 28, 2010. http://rhettandlinkommunity.com/m/discussion?id=2452419:Topic:86494.

Shaffer, Josh. "Rhett and Link's Forever Friendship, Bonded in Blood." *Raleigh News & Observer*, November 28, 2017. https://www.newsobserver.com/news/local/article186860328.html.

Stampler, Laura. "Meet The 25 Most Creative People in Advertising: 2012." *Business Insider*, July 14, 2012. https://www.businessinsider.com/the-most-creative-people-in-advertising-2012-7?op=1.

Testa, Chuck. "Official Ojai Valley Taxidermy TV Commercial." YouTube, August 14, 2011. https://youtu.be/LJP1DphOWPs.

USC School of Cinematic Arts. "Digital Troubadours." YouTube, April 15, 2009. https://youtu.be/eQEtt1tEbv0.

INDEX

ABOUT THE AUTHOR

Kerry Hinton is a writer and aspiring voiceover artist. He also plays the guitar but has yet to record a viral comedy song with millions of views. In the early 2000s, he had a one-line role in a Bravo TV comedy pilot. Unfortunately, the network did not order additional episodes. Like Rhett and Link, Kerry enjoys sketch comedy, songwriting, and podcasts. He lives in Brooklyn, New York, with his smart TV and a cat named Chicken.

PHOTO CREDITS